Short Stories for Students, Volume 4

Staff

Editorial: Kathleen Wilson, Marie Lazzari, *Editors.* Greg Barnhisel, Thomas Bertonneau, Cynthia Bily, Paul Bodine, Julia Burch, Yoonmee Chang, John Chua, Carol Dell'Amico, Catherine Dominic, Mark Elliot, Terry Girard, Rena Korb, Rebecca Laroche, *Sketchwriters.* Suzanne Dewsbury, James Person, *Contributing Editors.* Aarti Stephens, *Managing Editor*

Research: Victoria B. Cariappa, *Research Manager.* Andrew Malonis, *Research Specialist.*

Permissions: Susan M. Trosky, *Permissions Manager.* Kimberly Smilay, *Permissions Specialist.* Kelly Quin, *Permissions Associate.*

Production: Mary Beth Trimper, *Production Director.* Evi Seoud, *Assistant Production Manager.* Shanna Heilveil, *Production Assistant*

Graphic Services: Randy Bassett, *Image Database Supervisor*. Mikal Ansari, Robert Duncan, *Imaging Specialists*. Pamela A. Reed, *Photography Coordinator*.

Copyright Notice

This book is printed on acid-free paper that meets the minimum requirements of American National Standard for Information Sciences—Permanence Paper for Printed Library Materials, ANSI Z39.48-1984.

ISBN 0-7876-2219-2
ISSN 1092-7735

Printed in the United States of America
10 9 8 7 6 5 4 3 2 1

Lamb to the Slaughter

Roald Dahl 1953

Introduction

Initially rejected, along with four other stories, by *The New Yorker,* "Lamb to the Slaughter" eventually appeared in *Collier's* in 1953, after Knopf published its first collection of Dahl's short stories and established his American reputation. Dahl had been making headway as a professional writer with a spate of tales which, like "Lamb to the Slaughter," reflect aspects of human perversity, cruelty, and violence. "Lamb to the Slaughter" opens with Mary Maloney, the pregnant, doting wife of a policeman waiting for her husband to come home from work. When he does so, he makes an abrupt but unspecified statement to Mary, the upshot of which is that he intends to leave her. Her connubial complacency shattered by this revelation, Mary crushes her husband's skull with a frozen leg of lamb and then arranges an alibi. The laconic suddenness of the events, as Dahl tells them, creates an experience of shock for the reader, an effect which no doubt accounts for the popularity of this frequently anthologized and reprinted story. Dahl, who is also the author of popular childrens' fiction, appears here as an adult student of adult evil, as a cynically detached narrator, and as an advocate of a grisly form of black comedy. Yet "Lamb to the Slaughter" prefigures the grotesqueness in even his work for children: in both *James and the Giant Peach* and *Charlie and the Chocolate Factory* "bad" children meet with bizarre and horrific but appropriate fates.

Roald Dahl was born in Wales to Norwegian parents. His father died the year he was born, and his mother remained in Great Britain. He attended the prestigious Repton public preparatory school, where he was a quiet, bookish student, but never went on to college. After graduation, Dahl went to work for the Dutch Shell Oil company, and was posted overseas in Africa. At the outbreak of World War I in 1939, he joined the Royal Air Force and became a fighter pilot. Shot down during a sortie over Greece, Dahl was injured and spent the rest of the war in Washington DC, as a spy. Among his colleagues in the United States at the time was another future writer, the creator of James Bond, Ian Fleming.

Dahl published a highly embellished account of his war escapades in *Colliers* magazine in 1942, and started writing regularly after that, gradually gaining success. By the end of the 1950s, he was a successful and well-known author. With *James and the Giant Peach* (1961) and *Charlie and the Chocolate Factory* (1964) he also established himself as a writer for young people. In 1954 he married the film actress Patricia Neal. In part through Neal, he made acquaintances in the film industry and worked in Hollywood as a screen writer. His most famous screenplay may have been his adaptation of Fleming's James Bond novel *You Only Live Twice* (1967). He also adapted his own work for motion pictures, writing the screenplay for *Willy Wonka & the Chocolate Factory* (1971). Dahl died in 1990.

Plot Summary

Dahl commences with a picture of static coziness in a middle-class, domestic setting. Mary Maloney, six months pregnant, waits for her policeman husband Patrick Maloney to come home from work. The scene emphasizes domesticity: "The room was warm and clean, the curtains drawn." Matching chairs, lamps, glasses, and whisky, soda, and ice cubes await. Mary watches the clock, smiling quietly to herself as each minute brings her husband closer to home. When he arrives, she takes his coat and hangs it in the closet. The couple sits and drinks in silence—Mary comfortable with the knowledge that Patrick does not like to talk much until after the first drink. So by deliberate design, everything seems normal until Mary notices that Patrick drains most of his drink in a single swallow, and then pours himself another, very strong drink. Mary offers to fix dinner and serve it to him so that he does not have to leave his chair, although they usually dine out on Thursdays. She also offers to prepare a snack. Patrick declines all her offers of food. The reader becomes aware of a tension which escapes Mary's full notice.

Patrick confronts Mary and makes a speech, only the upshot of which is given explicitly: "So there it is. . . . And I know it's a kind of bad time to be telling you, but there simply wasn't any other way. Of course, I'll give you money and see you're looked after. But there needn't really be any fuss."

For reasons which Dahl does not make explicit, Patrick has decided to leave his pregnant wife.

Mary goes into shock. At first she wonders if she imagined the whole thing. She moves automatically to retrieve something from the basement freezer and prepare supper. She returns with a frozen leg of lamb to find Patrick standing by a window with his back to her. Hearing her come in, he tells her not to make supper for him, that he is going out. With no narrative notice of any emotional transformation, Mary walks up to him and brings the frozen joint of meat down "as hard as she could" on his head. Patrick falls dead.

She emerges from her shock to feel panic. Do the courts sentence pregnant women to death? Do they execute both mother and child? Do they wait until the tenth month? Not wanting to take a chance on her child's life, she immediately begins setting up an alibi. She puts the lamb in the oven to cook, washes her hands, and tidies her hair and makeup. She hurries to her usual grocery store, telling the grocer, Sam, that she needed potatoes and peas because Patrick did not want to eat out and she was "caught. . . without any vegetables in the house." In a moment of truly black comedy, the grocer asks about dessert: "How about afterwards? What are you going to give him for afterwards?" and she agrees to a slice of cheesecake. On her way home, she mentally prepares herself to be shocked by anything tragic or terrible she might find.

When she sees her husband's corpse again, she remembers how much she once loved him, and her tears of loss are genuine. She is sincerely distraught when she calls the local police station—the one where Patrick has worked—to report what she has found. Mary knows the policemen who report to the crime scene, and she casts Sergeant Jack Noonan in the role of her comforter. A doctor, police photographer, fingerprint expert, and two detectives join the investigation, while Noonan periodically checks on Mary. She tells her story again, from the beginning: Patrick came home, was too tired to go out for supper, so she left him relaxing at home while she started the lamb cooking and then ran out for vegetables. One detective checks with the grocer, who confirms Mary's account. No one seems to seriously consider her a suspect. The focus of the investigation in on finding the murder weapon—which must be a large, heavy blunt instrument. The detectives ask Mary about tools, and she professes ignorance but says that there may be some out in the garage. She remains in a chair while the house is searched.

Noonan tries to persuade Mary to stay somewhere else for the night, but she refuses. She asks him to bring her a drink and suggests that he have one too. Eventually all of the police investigators are standing around, sipping drinks, tired from their fruitless search. Noonan notices that the oven is still on and the lamb has finished cooking. Mary thanks him for turning the oven off and then asks her dead husband's gathered colleagues-knowing that they have worked long past their own mealtimes—to eat the dinner she had fixed for Patrick. She could not eat a thing, she tells them, but Patrick would want her to offer them "decent hospitality," especially as they are the men who will catch her husband's killer.

The final scene of the story concerns the policemen eating in the kitchen and discussing the case while Mary listens from the living room. The men agree that the killer probably discarded the massive murder weapon almost immediately, and predict that they will find it on the premises. Another theorizes that the weapon is probably "right under our very noses."

them, but Barnes would want us to offer them

The final sentence of the story forces the
reader to confront his own...
the Maloney household is the same...

Characters

Mary Moloney

Mary Maloney, the story's protagonist, is six months pregnant and satisfied with her (from an external perspective) rather banal life with her policeman-husband Patrick, whom she adores. She had "a slow smiling air about her" and was "curiously tranquil." Mary keeps a neat home, and busies herself with preparations for the baby. When Patrick unexpectedly announces that he is ending their marriage, Mary enters a state of shock. She automatically goes to the basement to remove something from the freezer for supper. She takes the first thing she finds—a leg of lamb—carries it back up the stairs, approaches her husband from behind, and strikes him on the head with the frozen leg of lamb. He falls to the floor dead. "The violence of the crash, the noise, the small table overturning, helped bring her out of the shock." Concern for the well-being of her coming child leads her to act quickly and efficiently to establish an alibi. She starts cooking the leg of lamb, rehearses a normal conversation with the grocer, and then goes to the store to buy vegetables. She hurries home, thinking that if "she happened to find anything unusual, or tragic, or terrible, then naturally it would be a shock and she'd become frantic with grief and horror." In fact, when she sees her husband's lifeless body again, she remembers her "love and longing for him" and cries over him quite sincerely. She then telephones her husband's police colleagues and collapses in a chair while they search the house for the "heavy blunt instrument, almost certainly a large piece of metal," that is believed to be the missing murder weapon. When a sergeant points out that the oven is still on and the leg of lamb is done, Mary urges the policemen—"good friends of dear Patrick's . . . helping to catch the man who killed him"—to eat it bercause she knows they have missed their own suppers. The policemen consume the murder weap-on on while speculating about the case. "And in the other room, Mary Maloney began to giggle."

Patrick Maloney

Patrick Maloney is a policeman still walking a beat. The reader learns that it is unusual for him to drain most of his evening cocktail in one swallow, as he does when he first comes home. He replies in short sentences or monosyllables as Mary watches him intently, trying to anticipate and fulfil his desires by offering to fix him another drink, bring his slippers, fix him a snack. He does not answer at all when Mary expresses her displeasure that "a policeman as senior as you" is still walking a beat— a suggestion that Patrick may not be especially successful at his job. On the evening of the story, Patrick abruptly announces that he is leaving Mary, although he will continue to provide for her financially. His only acknowlegement of her pregnancy is that he says he knows "it's kind of a bad time to be telling you." He hopes that there will be no fuss about it. Although the reader is told little outright about Patrick's character, the narrative implicitly indicates that he dislikes her worshipful adoration of him, her constant catering, and her tactless reminder about his lack of advancement in his profession.

Sergeant Jack Noonan

Noonan is one of the policemen at Patrick Maloney's precinct who responds to her frantic telephone call that she found her husband lying on the floor, apparently dead. He and Mary know one another, and he helps the weeping woman gently into a chair before joining another policeman in examining the body and scene and calling for other investigators. He is solicitous of Mary's well-being, asking if she would like to go and stay with a relative or with his own wife, or be helped up to bed. At one point she asks him to bring her a drink. He, and the remaining officers and detectives, also help themselves to whisky at her urging. It is the sergeant who notices that the oven is still on and the leg of lamb done cooking. Mary begs him and the others to eat the meal that she cannot bring herself to touch, and after some demurral, all the policemen sit down in the kitchen and completely devour the murder weapon.

O'Malley

O'Malley is Sergeant Noonan's partner. Dahl

is having fun with stereotypes, for O'Malley, like Maloney and Noonan, is an Irish name, and "the Irish cop" was a sociological phenomenon in American big cities in the late nineteenth and early twentieth centuries. O'Malley's words and actions are not specified in the story: he is just one of the policemen on the scene, discussing the case and, eventually, unwittingly consuming a portion of the tasty murder weapon.

Sam

Sam, the grocer, appears in the middle of the story. After Mary has killed Patrick, she constructs an alibi by making a hasty visit to the grocery store to buy vegetables to go with the meal she tells Sam she is cooking because Patrick does not want to eat out, as they usually do on Thursday nights. Mary later overhears a policeman reporting that Sam found her behavior at the store "quite normal."

Themes

Betrayal

"Lamb to the Slaughter" tells of at least one betrayal: Patrick Maloney's unexplained decision to leave his pregnant wife. This violation of the marriage-vow is obviously not the only betrayal in the story, however. Mary's killing of her husband is perhaps the ultimate betrayal. Her elaborately planned alibi and convincing lies to the detectives also constitute betrayal.

Identity

Dahl plays with the notion of identity both at the level of popular psychology and at a somewhat more philosophical, or perhaps anthropological, level. At the level of popular psychology, Dahl makes it clear through his description of the Maloney household that Mary has internalized the bourgeois, or middle class, ideal of a young mid-twentieth-century housewife, maintaining a tidy home and catering to her husband; pouring drinks when the man finishes his day is a gesture that comes from movies and magazines of the day. Mary's sudden murderous action shatters the image that we have of her and that she seems to have of herself. Dahl demonstrates, in the deadly fall of the frozen joint, that "identity" can be fragile. (Once she shatters her own identity, Mary must carefully reconstruct it for protective purposes, as when she sets up an alibi by feigning a normal conversation with the grocer.)

Topics for Further Study

- Examine the elements of the story that make it a black comedy. How does Dahl use irony to bring humor to the plot?

- "Lamb to the Slaughter" can be considered a revenge fantasy. Think of some other revenge fantasies you have read or seen in movies and on television shows. Write about how such stories can function as a catharsis. Think of a revenge fantasy you have had yourself and write it as a fictional story.

- What percentage of murders are

instances of domestic abuse? Does the unpremeditated nature of Mary's crime make it seem less horrible than if it had been planned? Do you think a person like Mary could really kill someone so suddenly?

- An old saying hold that "Revenge is a dish best served cold," meaning that if you want to take vengeance, you should wait and plan carefully and not act impulsively against the person who has wronged you. If Mary had consciously decided to avenge herself on her husband for deserting her, and waited and planned, do you think she would have killed him? What else might she have done to pay him back for his treatment of her?

In the anthropological sense, Dahl appears to suggest that, in essence, human beings are fundamentally nasty and brutish creatures capable of precipitate and bloody acts. Then there are the police detectives, who pride themslves on their ability to solve a crime, but whom Mary sweetly tricks into consuming the main exhibit. Their identity, or at least their competency, is thrown into doubt.

Love and Passion

At the beginning of "Lamb to the Slaughter," Mary Maloney feels love and physical passion for her husband Patrick. She luxuriates in his presence, in the "warm male glow that came out of him to her," and adores the way he sits, walks, and behaves. Even far along into her pregnancy, she hurries to greet him, and waits on him hand and foot —much more attentively, it appears from his reactions, than he would like. Patrick is presumably motivated to leave his wife by an overriding passion for something or someone else. Mary's mention of his failure to advance at work, and his own wish that she not make a "fuss" about their separation because "It wouldn't be very good for my job" indicate that it may be professional success that he desires. His treatment of his wife does not suggest that he loves her.

Passivity

The concept of passivity figures in the story. The first pages of the story portray Mary's existence as almost mindlessly passive: she sits and watches the clock, thinking that each minute brings her husband closer to her. She is content to watch him closely and try to anticipate his moods and needs. Patrick's predictability up to this point is part of this passivity. The two are living a clockwork life against which, in some way, each ultimately rebels. Passivity appears as the repression of passion, and passion finds a way to reassert itself.

Justice and Injustice

The question of justice and injustice is directly related to the question of revenge. "Lamb to the Slaughter" narrates a train of injustices, beginning with Patrick's betrayal of Mary and their marriage, peaking with Mary's killing of Patrick, and finding its denouement in Mary's deception of the investigating officers. Patrick acts unjustly (or so it must be assumed on the basis of the evidence) in announcing his abandonment of Mary, for this breaks the wedding oath; Mary acts unustly, in a way far exceeding her husband's injustice, in killing Patrick, and she compounds the injustice by concealing it from the authorities.

Black Humor

Black humor is the use of the grotesque, morbid, or absurd for darkly comic purposes. Black humor became widespread in popular culture, especially in literature and film, beginning in the 1950s; it remains popular toward the end of the twentieth century. Joseph Heller's novel *Catch-22* (1961) is one of the best-known examples in American fiction. The short stories of James Thurber and the stories and novels of Kurt Vonnegut, Jr. also offer examples. The image of the cheerful housewife suddenly smashing her husband's skull with the frozen joint of meat intended for his dinner is itself blackly humorous for its unexpectedness and the grotesque incongruity of the murder weapon. There is a morbid but funny double meaning, too, in Mary's response to her grocer's question about meat: "I've got meat, thanks. I got a nice leg of lamb from the freezer." She did indeed get a leg of lamb from the freezer, and after she used it as a club, she found herself with a rather large portion of dead meat on her living-room floor. Also darkly funny is the grocer's question about what she plans to give her husband "afterwards," that is, for dessert. From Mary's point of view, Patrick has already gotten his "just desserts," and there will be no more "afterwards" for him! The ultimate example of black humor in "Lamb to the Slaughter" is, of course, the spectacle of the policemen and detectives sitting around the Maloney kitchen table, speculating about the murder weapon while they unwittingly devour it.

Point of View

Dahl grants the point of view to Mary, the protagonist. Right away, readers see the scene through Mary's eyes. The warmth and cleanliness, the punctilious ordiliness, of the living room where Mary awaits Patrick reflect Mary's conviction, soon to be shattered, that she has built a comfortable and even beautiful life. In Patrick's case, Dahl communicates indirectly by gesture. Mary greets Patrick with a "Hullo, Darling," while Patrick responds with a "hullo" only, omitting the endearment. He drinks his evening scotch and soda more quickly than usual and resists Mary's efforts to wait on him; he fails to respond to Mary's conversation. Readers see these things more or less as Mary sees them, although they likely interpret them more quickly than she does as signs of his dissatisfaction with his marriage. After the killing, Mary changes. No longer the ornament of a contented setting, she becomes the calculator of her own survival, and that of her unborn child. As Dahl writes, Mary's mind suddenly clears; she begins to dispose of evidence, and she sits in front of her dresser-mirror rehearsing a normal conversation with her grocer. When she returns home, having founded her alibi, she views the body of her husband as if for the first time, and readers, too, get a newish view of it, described much more grotesquely, with greater and more poignant detail, than previously. In these two contrasting scenes of the death, Dahl completes the transformation of his central character.

Symbols

The setting is symbolic: Its domestic primness implies Mary's having bought into a rather banal version of middle class happiness. The frozen leg of lamb is also symbolic and indeed constitutes the central symbol of the story. The piece of meat is already a token of violence: an animal traditionally viewed as meek and gentle slaughtered for carnivorous consumption. The notion of a lamb, moreover, resonates with biblical symbols, such as the scapegoat mentioned in Leviticus, the ram that substitutes for Isaac in the tale of Abraham and Isaac, or Jesus himself, "the Lamb of God." But Dahl's story reverses the connotation of these biblical images.

Historical Context

The Post-War Decade

Dahl began his writing career in 1942 with a story about being shot down while fighting in North Africa. Violence, whether associated with warfare or with crime, continued to fascinate Dahl and figures prominently even in his childrens' stories. "Lamb to the Slaughter" belongs to the first full decade of Dahl's writing career and to the first decade of what historians call the Post-War period. This period witnessed the sociological and cultural transformation of the Western world and took hold as strongly in the United States, where Dahl had come to live, as in Europe. Among the features of the Post-War period may be tallied the growth of cities and the attendant rise in urban tension, the incipient liberation of women, young people, and minorities, the sense that the normative, agriculturally based America that had existed up until the nation's involvement in World War II was in radical dissolution. It is significant with respect to Dahl's story that divorce, formerly rare in the statistics of American life, began to rise in the aftermath of the war.

Compare & Contrast

- **1950s:** Precisely because the

traditional social norms had begun to come under the pressures that would lead to change, American society in the 1950s tended to reaffirm the norms of religion, family, self-reliance, law and order, and strongly defined gender roles.

1990s: Certain social trends only barely visible in 1950 now present themselves glaringly: the statistical likelihood that many marriages will fail, for example, and the ubiquitousness of violent crime. Restrictive gender roles are one of the most frequently attacked social mores in the late twentieth century. Murder is commonplace and horrific domestic violence abounds. For example, in the mid-1980s, a suburban Detroit, Michigan man killed his wife and kept her body in a locked freezer for several years, until one of the couple's daughters discovered it.

- **1953:** Simone de Beauvoir's nonfiction study of 1949 denouncing the unequal position of women in most public and private arenas is published in translation in the United States as *The Second Sex*.

1990s: Women still earn, on average, only 75% of what similarly educated men earn in comparable positions.

- **1950s:** The English and American populations, recovering from two wars (World War II and the Korean War), responded enthusiastically to economic trends, embracing the new standard of cheap housing and abundant material goods within the price-range of middle-class "consumers."

  1990s: The "baby boom" generation (those born in the post-World War II years) is the first in English and American history to be measurably worse off financially than their parents generation.

Popular Fiction

The same decade was also the heyday of popular fiction in the United States, with dozens of weekly and monthly journals featuring short fiction and serialized novels, and with paperback publishing getting under way. Dahl began his career in the "weeklies" before breaking into print in commercial book form. The wave of popular fiction, emphasizing the short story, saw the differentiation of genres. Police and detective fiction, war fiction, science fiction, romance, even the business story, all represent distinct genres which appealed to well-defined groups of readers.

Television Culture

The year of "Lamb to the Slaughter," 1953, puts the story in the glory days of American television, on which at the time gimmicky dramas of a slightly grotesque character frequently appeared. (Rod Serling's *Twilight Zone,* which would come along in 1957, represented the zenith of the trend.) With its two-setting structure (the Maloney household and the counter of a grocery store) and its limited dramatis personae, "Lamb to the Slaughter" has the feel of a teleplay scenario. The black comedy and the opportunity for potential viewers to be in the know while certain characters (the detectives) remain ignorant of the facts, also conform to the nature of the one-act, half-hour TV drama interrupted by commercial messages.

Critical Overview

The critical reception of Dahl's story "Lamb to the Slaughter" needs to be put in the context of his critical reception generally. First of all, Dahl achieved commercial success, and after a period of struggle, became wealthy on the basis of his writing. For this to happen, a writer must have talent and he must have a sense of how to make that talent appeal to large numbers of ordinary readers. There is, moreover, often a difference between what a large segment of the literate public wants and what academically trained editors, who stand between authors and the public, think that the public wants or what the public ought to want. Once his writing reached its audience, Dahl never experienced any difficulty; before reaching his audience, at the editorial level, however, Dahl often confronted obstacles. "Lamb to the Slaughter" was originally rejected by *The New Yorker* in 1951. In the meantime, Dahl had established contact with the publishing firm of Knopf, which brought out a collection of his previously published stories called *Someone Like You* in 1953. This collection was successful with the American reading public. Unpublished Dahl stories were now sought by magazines, and *Colliers* ran the stories that *The New Yorker* had rejected, including "Lamb to the Slaughter."

Critical reaction to Dahl's first published collection, summarized by Jeremy Treglown in a biography of the author, makes the case. *Someone Like You* received a good number of reviews, the majority favorable, a few condescending; but even the favorable ones tended to categorize Dahl as a strictly popular writer. Treglown quotes *New York Times* critic James Kelly praising Dahl as "the *compleat* short-story writer." Yet Kelly went on to differentiate classes of short-story specialists. On the one hand there are writers like Chekhov, the Russian, an indubitable artist and explorer of human psychological depth; on the other hand, there are "solid plotters like Saki, O. Henry, Maupassant and Maugham" to which latter category he assigns Dahl. "The reader looking for sweetness, light, and subtle characterization will have to try another address," Kelly wrote. Among the negative reviews, one from the *Buffalo News* opined that even though he was a beginning author, Dahl was unlikely to achieve much in the way of a higher level of artistic expression; the same reviewer disliked Dahl's stories for their unrelievedly sardonic attitude and for their lack of social significance. Nevertheless, as Treglown notes, "by Christmas [1953], 7500 hundred copies had been sold."

"Lamb to the Slaughter" benefited from the success of *Someone Like You,* and Dahl quickly marketed it to *Colliers.* The story has been widely reprinted ever since. As Treglown writes, the story of Mary Maloney's murder of her husband constitutes "a comic crime thriller in miniature which was to become one of [Dahl's] best-known stories and whose plot must be among the first to depend on a domestic freezer." Notice that

Treglown refers to the story as "comic," stressing its black humor. Treglown makes a virtue of what other critics of Dahl have seen as a vice, namely a penchant for the grotesque and a nasty vision of human existence. This divergence of opinion sums up the critical reaction to Dahl rather neatly.

As he gradually deemphasized "adult" fiction in favor of "children's stories" in the late 1950s and early 1960s, Dahl found that, despite the popularity of such items as *Charlie and the Chocolate Factory,* some academic students of "children's stories" did not approve of him. It was thought that an amoral viciousness undermined the moral order in Dahl's chilcren's fiction. In its elements of savagery and rejection of the rules of behavior, "Lamb to the Slaughter" might be described as a "childrens' story for adults."

What Do I Read Next?

- Dahl's first published story, "Shot

Down over Libya," appeared in *Saturday Evening Post* in August 1942. As Dahl's earliest work, it merits the attention of anyone interested in the remainder of his stories. The story stems from Dahl's experience in the Royal Air Force, heavily fictionalized, and introduces the element of violence which threads through his oeuvre. A pilot, a British flying his Hurricane in support of ground troops, meets up with an aerial ambush by Italian aircraft, which shoot him into the ground. He survives the crash, but is injured. Despite its slightness, "Shot Down" prefigures much of the later writing.

- The short stories of Kurt Vonnegut, Jr., collected in *Welcome to the Monkey House,* have been cited in comparison with those of Dahl for their darkly comic nature and often bleak assessments of human nature.

- In Dahl's story "The Way Up To Heaven," a woman is infuriated by her husband's chronic lateness. She begins to suspect that he is late deliberately to torment her. She siezes a chance opportunity to leave him stranded in a disabled elevator where he will almost certainly die.

- For many years, Dahl was married to the actress Patricia Neal, whose autobiography *As I Am* (1988) contains a frank depiction of their life together and of the factors that drove them apart.

- In James Thurber's short story "Mr. Preble Gets Rid of His Wife," a typically mild-mannered, married Thurber protagonist had an ongoing joke with a female colleague about running away together. One day she varies her standard response by saying that first he will have to "get rid of" his wife. That night Mr. Preble lures his wife into the cellar of their home, planning to kill her and bury the body under the earthen floor. She is reluctant to enter the cellar, but once she does, she realizes what he plans to do. She belittles his plan, criticizes his choice of a murder weapon, and mocks his general ineptitude as a prospective murderer. The story ends with Mrs. Preble sending him away to find a more suitable weapon and screaming after him to "close the door . . . were you born in a barn?"

- *A Modest Proposal* by Jonathan Swift is an early and famous example of literary irony and grotesque humor. Under its full title: *A Modest Proposal for Preventing the Children of the Poor People from Being a Burthen to Their Parents, or the Country, and for Making them Beneficial to the Publick,* the essay shocked some members of the public when it appeared in 1729, advocating that problems of famine, poverty, and overpopulation be addressed by eating the children of the poor.

Sources

Treglown, Jeremy. *Roald Dahl: A Biography.* New York: Farrar Strauss & Giroux, 1994, p. 105.

Further Reading

Raphael, Frederic. "Stories from the Source of Heartlessness." *The Times Literary Supplement,* No. 4618, October 4, 1991, p. 28.

> An assessment of Dahl's career, noting that he was a mass-market writer but comparing him to some of the finest prose stylists of the twentieth century. Raphael theorizes that Dahl's war experiences as a fighter pilot, which he wrote about in the stories collected in Over to You, are responsible for the bitterness and cruelty of much of his later fiction.

Warren, Alan. *Roald Dahl.* Mercer Island, Wash.: Starmont, 1988, 105 p.

> Critical study of Dahl's fiction, including a chapter on filmed adaptations of his stories.

West, Mark I. *Roald Dahl.* N.Y.: Twayne, 1992, 148 p.

> Biographical and critical study, covering Dahl's life and literary career.

CPSIA information can be obtained
at www.ICGtesting.com
Printed in the USA
LVHW081524020919
629657LV00015B/2057/P